Ripening

Ripening

Paul Hunter

Silverfish Review Press
Eugene, Oregon

ACKNOWLEDGMENTS

Thanks are due to the editors of the following publications, where some of these poems first appeared: *Small Farmer's Journal, Square Lake, Weathered Pages: The Poetry Pole* (Blue Begonia Press), and *The Wandering Hermit Review.*

Published by
Silverfish Review Press
P.O. Box 3541
Eugene, OR 97403
www.silverfishreviewpress.com

Distributed by
Small Press Distribution
800-869-7553
orders@spdbooks.org
www.spdbooks.org

Library of Congress Cataloging-in-Publication Data

Hunter, Paul, 1943-
  Ripening : poems / by Paul Hunter. --1st ed.
    p. cm.
  ISBN 978-1-878851-52-9
  I. Title.

PS3558.U487R57 2007
811'.54--dc22

                                        2006102341

Manufactured in the United States of America

In memory of
Edwin Gaynor
John Andres
& William Ward

Table of Contents

I. The Mystery

What a Boy Lies Awake Wondering

Footsore trudging these fields
while overhead dip and wheel
unfolding lives on the wing
some evenings every other living thing
seems dipped in desire glistening

so I envy the horse that can ripple
its skin out from under the horsefly
and the thousand-eyed horsefly
that bites me clean through
the workshirt stuck to my shoulders

I envy the hen so suspicious
of me she can turn her head backwards
and the slippery calf being nudged up
licked clean of its birth
all set to dance at a touch

and the water skeeter astride
the silvery skin of the horse trough
inhaled by those whiskery muzzles
and the green snake so still in the lilac
whose tongue neatly scissors the world

Chore to Begin and End Work

Now ladies come along
Edwin calls and they follow
Hetty Bridey and Brindle
Sister Dolly and Velvet

ushered into the parlor
order always the same
sleepwalking nodding
clop across clean wetted concrete
swollen udders tolling
the time for them always known

heads lowered munching alfalfa
willing necks thrust into stocks
knowing embrace of the hobbles
screech of the stool drawn close
feel of the hands warmed in armpits
that close down each teat
raising faint plumes
steaming the chill air

occasional switch of the tail
stamp heave kick
shove back against the ear
held to her side for the warmth
that can't miss the song of content
churning the four great stomachs

chore to begin and end work
with clean calloused hands
twice a day 5 and 5
wed to these fourteen kept fresh
with never a day a night off

their sweet white substance a living
meditation a summons a prayer
ritual squeeze alternating
rhythm rinsing rinsing
the side of the silver pail
burden eased hope slowly mounting
till the brides are turned out to pasture
and the foaming warm gallons pour

Steeplejack

Before the Fuller Brush Man
there would be fellows come round
tinkers to mend pots and pans
sharpen what have you

drummers peddlers
flogging the World Book of Knowledge
white covered Bibles
all manner of nostrums and flummeries

but the one itinerant artist wandering
backroads outside a circus
that caught the eye of the boys
around here was the steeplejack

who never mind hydraulic cherrypickers
steel scaffolding snaps together
these days in a matter of minutes
to safely get you up there

they heard tell was a sailor
used to working the rigging of ships
tall as the pines they are made of
and had truly been round the world

who would take a couple boards and ropes
a ladder for the easy part
a canvas bag for his tools
climb up patch that leak

without a net or prayer
creep in slow-motion
up to the point of the spire
take in the view all round like it was nothing

tighten that wobbly cross
shingle the highest windiest
peak they should maybe never
thought to have built in the first place

What Did I Know

Maybe it was young inexperienced
maybe old and frail
maybe it was a boy showing off
maybe a fleeing girl

but one bright November afternoon
without any others about
this squirrel ran to the naked
flexible ends of one tree

out to where the lattice tends to filigree
that ends in empty reaching
that bends with the slightest airs
beneath the slenderest body

lept for the arms of another
clutched at scrambled and missed
its outflung fingerlings
fell to the leaves with a thump

I ran to see perhaps help
the squirrel where it lay
mother grandparent child
teenager dropped from the sky

all one until my approach
it started up out of fear
scrambled into the bushes
crackling as if on fire

Through Fence Slats

Every country kid that has witnessed
the mystery knows
pawing and snorting the male's
blind rage that makes the ground shake
his intimidating show
the female's passive sidelong look
her lowered head once mounted
her insistent backing up

both in a dangerous dance
no one should come between
vulnerable once begun
oblivious to the others
circling in attendance
locked an instant
all too soon head flung
a roar of agony ended

fresh leaves in the clutch of
the first warm wind of spring
who knows what
makes them swirl
rear and press on as if
more than anything they desired
this madness to pass
this thunderstorm to be done

Bower

At thirteen Georgianna built a bower
of sumac sassafras dogwood
in a thicket below the cemetery

where did she get the notion
A Midsummer Night's Dream
maybe Spenser or Sidney

to bend around a ring of saplings
head to foot tie them down
weave into kind of a lattice

in and out out and in
shape like an airy bread loaf
or cage with a magical entrance

a crown that wouldn't shed water
or quite keep you warm
though it would offer shade

a nest you could crawl into
that might in time grow together
which is all she had in mind

but then the first time she spread
a picnic blanket to show
her secret place to a friend

a boy who had shadowed these girls
that she knew craved attention
though no clue how to begin

waited until they crept in
jumped on the roof and broke through
cookies lemonade everything

crushed the party
to which he had not been invited
her green living dream into nothing

shattered young trees in a ring
left to heal free of bindings
never dreamt of in daylight again

Wash Tub Saturday Night

Not always Saturday but mostly
when the tub clanks in from the shed
where from one week to the next
it hangs up out of the way

till the curtain gets pulled in the pantry
as the stovetop kettles and pots
steam up the windows
so little need now for drapes

the air gets sultry and hot
as we dig out our clean clothes
study our blisters and bruises
get ourselves ready to wash

with the kitchen lamps all ablaze
the hand mirror passing around
a little snipping and scraping
away the worst before and after

as in no particular order
depending mainly on need
one at a time we slip in
past the curtain strip and shiver

crouch naked in the tub
lather ourselves in all the hairy parts
then at last call out to another
to splash warm water down over us

as we lean back eyes closed
cleansed head to toe
as if in a modest baptism
rinse off the last of what ails us

and when all have had their turn
shared that feeling pounds lighter
hair a fragrant blossom of the head
drag the full tub sloshing to the door

heave out into the night
the week's dirt and exhaustion
where for a while in the yard
it steams and shines

Hayride

Into the chilly night air
under this light load piled high
harness for once purely music
no need for bells

with eight great shod
dinnerplate hooves
that clatter and ring over gravel
chime the tall iron-rimmed wheels

a lark for the old team hitched up
slumbering led from stalls
offered a few cider apples
their step a rare bounce and shuffle

swinging lanterns behind and above
as the team snorts bright plumes
and strikes sparks
under a full harvest moon

spread on the land
laid to rest a pale blanket
kids burrowed deep in new hay
tickling and tussling

some couples just of an age
begin what the old ones call sparking
inches apart now turn shy
lean back to study stars reeling

savor the dark the late hour
no matter come daylight tomorrow
most will have already risen
chores before starting to school

Edwin perched there up ahead
silent back turned against hearing
the young ones muffled in clover
smoldering nearly aglow

a swelling musical murmur
that all at once breaks out in song
that taken up hovers and carries
that bears us all the way home

Tomcatting

How's a boy supposed to go
take up an interest in girls
tomcat all around the countryside
share an ice cream skinnydip
swing in the shade play croquet
try out all the little byways
see where else they might take him

when his folks can stare off and see
whatever's coming for miles
even without work that can run
dawn till past dark down the longest of days

if not by overlooking
an occasional late rising
or nap in the hay with the barn cats
stumble and slump at the hoe

or given keys to the pickup
taking that run into town
on the flimsiest of excuses
overlook how the hours drag on
till the dust plume and roar
announce his belated return

Horse Knows the Way

Before the automobile was even dreamt of
with all its backfiring danger expense
blow-outs breakdowns running out of gas
couples going courting
off into a buggy late at night

forget excuses knew of
advantages long since overlooked
of a good horse where you didn't hardly need
to touch a rein never mind the whip or brake

forget one-hand driving
it could see better than you
even moonless nights anyhow
and wasn't looking backward
so you could do as you pleased

and knowing the way would go along
sleepwalking toward home forever

maybe slow here and there for a mouthful
but turn in right where it's sposed to
at the barn stand stamping and nodding
till somehow it woke you both
before the rising sun
could become an embarrassment

Padiddle

One fluttering yellow light
weaves toward you head-on
down a narrow country road

that folks thought to make
a game of flirtation and laughter
siphon off some of that fear

game of couples out riding
where the first to spot one says
padiddle gets to claim a kiss

still you can't help but wonder
what is it tractor motorsickle
maybe dim enough to be
a buggy clopping along
on one candlepower

most likely just a car
missing one headlight
since they practically never
burn out the same instant
though they always
try to sell a whole new pair

and there you are
caught deciding which is it
looming toward you
out of the dark left or right
how far should you pull over

and when will it be safe
to steal or plant
that kiss you earned just right

Barn Dance

Threshing floor a dull gleam
swaying paper lanterns hung
onlookers gathered around
each one scrubbed to begin

planted for now a wallflower
stricken impossibly shy
study the fiddler tuning
admire the banjo guitar

envy those with anything
useful to do with their hands
anywhere to rest their gaze
but sidewise on that special one

till taken with quickening music
the boldest girl leaps up
drags someone into the clearing
forgets her left feet starts to move

stomps till the rest feeling left out
sidle forth onto the floor
allow themselves to be carried
away where the partnering matters

less than the dancing partaken
to lend feet wings steel the backbone
somehow loosen the tongue
make the feast of this evening

linger not finish too soon
for never mind how each is led
tongue-tied to this enclosure
fears to be saddled and broken

though only gentled by night's end
what else is learned from
working outdoors in all weather
but the bloom lasts a moment

that times when nothing is growing
you will brood over crave
taste even trampling underfoot
what you would pluck out of love

Light and Air

In a fit of something no one need confess
maybe how a man faces one day
in the mirror sees he has slipped
past the point of attraction to anyone
into confirmed bachelorhood

Uncle Clyde finally tipped over
the old outhouse on his mother's place
shoveled it empty and spread
on a stand of young christmas trees
told her use the chamberpot for once

then went from hipboots at sunup
to hammering sweeping out cobwebs
sawhorses splinters and sawdust
one long day spent renovating
nailed down a fresh plank floor

a tight new shingle roof
put in a real sash window
and as he stood it back up
gave the whole thing a quarter turn
that should anybody ask

he never said just looked out on his fields
to lend the pungent business light and air
rather than leave the door wide for
the old woman to sneak up and catch
him reading true detective magazines

where you finger slick pictures in front
then tear out and wipe yourself
on the soft pulpy pages in back
where the stories all run together
in-between the advertisements

II. Getting By

The Work Nobody Loves

Before you even get to the prickly part
with the come-along hammer pliers
the job that'll chew through
a new pair of gloves eat your hands

first there is the plan
all the counting pacing off
pencil stub working numbers
out on a paper bag
then cutting eight-foot locust posts
lopping peeling stacking
then digging post holes
a bite at a time that'll get you
under the armpits
forearms elbows lower back

before you cut loose the roll
that uncoiling starts to bite
every which way like a snake

that nobody ever loved
except maybe Joe Glidden
who made a fortune peddling
such bundled cussedness

but fencing brandnew from scratch
is the least of it

mostly what you get
tree limbs blown down a storm
a couple posts rotted out
line of barbed wire let go
when you are smack in the middle
of doing anything else
just sat down to dinner
laid back on the pillow
when you most needed rest
there are your cows down the road
into the neighbor's alfalfa

and in the dark in the downpour up you get
knowing there is no such thing as half a fence
especially the other end of your pasture
down along the creek
livestock inspect every foot
knowing a fence is a bluff
any cow horse or hog could
run through knock down
if they didn't mind scratching themselves
getting their prideful tail tangled up

so you patch till it's halfway convincing
not worth the trouble running off
then round up the fugitives
doing this work of containment
we all hate like you meant it
till sunrise you can come back fix it right

Though the Almanac Says It's Too Late

We plant a quarter acre in tomatoes
down one edge of a field
already disked and plowed
already warm June ground
in a mad rush to be done

one goes along with the axle
every three-four feet lets drop
the other pokes a six-inch start
gently kicks dirt in its face
practically steps on it

then from the bucket each gets
a dipper of water no more
so much for babysitting
maybe once again we'll dash along
after weeds with a hoe

everything done such a hurry
yet hardly one fails to thrive
vines sprawled out all around
bear so heavily we run
clean out of baskets counter space

pick only the most luscious
about to burst of their own weight
past sunset lift red hands sore backs
in wonder that such abundance
should answer our haste and neglect

Silage

That summer too little too late
brings another lesson
in make-do and get-by
how to avert a disaster
approaching in slow motion
under cool cloudy skies
by acting quick as a thunderclap

how to mow rake and chop
acres of stunted young corn
still tasseling earing out
still reaching up with
no thought to tomorrow
cold and grey as today
how to murder your own crop

even without a real silo
makeshift pile in a trench
all that green on black plastic
stack straw bales all around
pull another sheet over
fold tight and tuck close
pile truck tires on top

against winter winds when
you will be thankful to dig
under snow to unwrap
fork a ripe steaming mouthful
of anything to still the lowing cattle
that eat till they stagger
drunk never do put on weight

This Failure

Say spring too wet for plowing
runs axle-deep into July
or the August oven never quite fires up
before an early killing frost

say it rains the whole summer
or you catch root mold or blight
go a parching year without a drop

There you stand in the field
one with all the others
frail tottering headless at a loss

though still with work to be done
to clear away or turn under
mow rake and burn off this failure
if there is to be another crop

Where Mostly Each Works Alone

How do you calculate
what you are fixing to do
when to plant what
whether to feed sell hold onto
root out or just cultivate

without you run into town
maybe once a week
spend half a rainy morning
over coffee at the café
plus Sundays after church

around that big back table where
the sheriff is usually parked
the one big chair with both arms
radio one hand conducting
county business while you listen in
everything else going on

though sometimes decent weather
with others nowhere about
you have to go make the rounds
of the likeliest places
loaf in shade alongside
courthouse hangers-on
check gas pump grocery parking lot
drift out by the grain elevator
gather around someone's pickup
to admire his precious load of scrap

or final resort go and visit
in the midst of whatever they're doing
one by one see what's what
which is how some manage best
picking the brains of another
like walnuts run down the driveway
no one seems to mind you help yourself

Something for Nothing

In town you hire a guy to do a thing
he does you pay him end of story
maybe takes forever charges
an arm and a leg even after
you show him the right way still
screws it up royally but

Twelve miles out from a crossroads
a hundred from the big city
say you got a muddy lane goes down
a little dip through deep woods
edge of a pond climbs a curve
perfect trap for a car all four seasons
with nowhere to turn around
no other way out no getting
a decent run at it you so much as spit
that yellow clay is syrup
man you're stuck

So you call up a fellow
in the skinny phonebook
under Heavy Construction
boasts demolition house moving
cisterns foundations dams bridges
figure he could maybe do a road
comes out for a look says
eighteen truck loads
of crick rock should do her
and ditch both sides for the runoff

You say fine shake hands
he says he'll get to it when he can
but for a few jobs ahead of you
you say we need to get in there
I mean half a mile to a tractor
every other time we get stuck
he says I take your point

A week later a road grader appears
one morning ditches both sides
then a dump truck makes seven trips
to the nearest crick that
no one cares who belongs to
a loader feeds gravel all sizes
basketballs wagon wheels dinner plates
hauls it back dumps seven piles
the grader runs down
to spread out and bust up the worst

And that is it for three years
the road grader sits there in weeds
alongside the half-finished road
that works about like you'd expect
rough but so what

Till one day the grader evaporates
never a bill and not another word
though like the man said
he'd see what he could do

And who knows what it's about
some of the local boys figure
maybe a borrowed road grader
with borrowed license plates
needing a safe spot to hide
off the side of a side road
till someone died or forgot
what everyone knows not to ask

Tough to Kill

Never mind he's not much of a farmer
crops go in weeks after the rest
make up the verge of first frost

or that twenty miles off he can point to
a crossroads still bears his name
last of a long-known family
that drew the map on these parts

Nick may be the original hopeless case
learned to run a still at his daddy's knee
acquired an aversion to school
a craving for drink by fourth grade
took up one let go the other
no one to say any different

though once booze was legal
too much like a job to keep
burying digging up hauling
around in the dark all his works
copper coil and pot slobber bucket
all those cases of jars
so mostly his business dried up

like the best of the boys he went off
did something in the war
he never much talks about
got him shot to pieces patched up

so mostly he just gets by
keeps what he calls lubricated
pours the juice down checks for leaks

and when county cops towed
what was left of his car
back up where it threaded through trees
mowed forty feet of good fence
where he blacked out at the wheel
bulldozed deep in high corn come to rest

understandably took his license
locked him up but since
he lives a good ways out of town
place of his own where
they have to pretend to leave
him a way to make a living
if not the means to get around

these days he navigates
the back roads at twelve miles an hour
on that International Harvester
one ugly lump of grease and oil
rusted past redemption
mud and manure welded to it
with water and ethylene glycol
in the rear tires for the traction
just like him tough to kill

that takes a good hour and a half
to run in to the tavern
the same home past dark
with one wavering yellow padiddle
a ragged clatter standing in the road
where he stops to piss reconnoiter
weave a little singsong to himself
that should you ever come across
wave and give a wide berth

Like Nick's Tractor

Age wear and tear compound troubles
that slip up on you
like Nick's tractor

that still pulls fine on a level
that with a full load can climb
practically any hill he comes upon

though going down the other side
as the old folks will tell you
is a whole other matter

it likes to pop out of gear
and with its feeble shuddering brakes
lose control and run away with him

he should see it coming every time
but you know how most of us
live in hope

and not of the resurrection
so rather than tearing it down
to replace the worn gears and shaft

he cusses the old thing
that will never change for the better
and calls it pure luck

to get down off that hillside
between trees
that keep jumping up in his path

Beaten Path

When all is gone and done
door slammed rattling home
the real driving lessons still come
along back roads you tear
down an endless dumptruck pour
of gravel slushing the silence
high noon rocking dead level
or midnight frozen griddle
dust or snow plume billowing aloft

yes gravel back roads that turn
from two lane to one lane to dirt
where you learn not to barrel blindly
so as to meet up the hard way
but feel your way around curves

where you mostly learn to eat dust
drive in ruts follow others
and only where wheels cut too deep
mean bottomless mud loss of traction
where the highside hogback may
scrape and clutch your underbelly

there you learn to sashay
up out of the morass
straddle spine and shoulder
lurch along lean to one side
through this closing hole in green curtains
this leafy wall brushing past
underneath overhead otherwise

pure expression of being
in a blind hurry now slowed
to a dreamy push
caress of the riffling changes
on through the tunnel of now

until your way ends
amid chickens ducks someone's yard
on the porch a loud dog

or else drains off and firms up again
meanders rivers mounts hills
as the old endless road leads you back
to the blinking lights fourway stops printed signs
run-arounds speed traps cul-de-sacs
of so-called civilization

In the Midst of Great Doubt

Somewhere along in the depression
in the midst of great doubt
a fellow come around said
he'd cover the sides of your house
in crick rock for eighty dollars
in town a good man's month's wages
never mind what farm hands got
said it would hold in heat
shut out cold so you'd never
have to paint which none did
anyhow those days in these parts

so one old boy took him up on it
went to hauling rock by the wagonload
while the man got started
dug a trench laid in gravel
then leaned in foundation stones
then started laying sideways slabs
up three-four inches thick
using galvanized nails
to hold while mortar hardened
raised up a rickety scaffold
lifting up fitting together
some of the huge dinner plates
a hundred-fifty pounds four feet around
every other one showing
crick bed fossils from back when
all this was once an ocean

so even if it's not a work of art
there is always something to look at
even should it fail an education

and they were all amazed
covering two full storeys
only took three days
he was so hardworking so chipper
what with his endless whistling
and the tink-tink of his hammer
they were a little disappointed
once he got paid and lit out

after which they watched and waited
mostly expecting the worst
though twenty-five years later
it still looked pretty good
except for a little crumbling
the hardest places to get at
up under the eaves
just about where you'd expect
the first nail to rust out

Blue-Black

In twilight lavender fading to blue-black
I would go down by the crick with my shotgun
the cheapest kind of 20 gauge single-shot
with a hammer you had to cock

pick up a pebble
in my left hand toss it up
and one of the bats feeding on the bugs
rising in the cool air over water

would swoop after it
realize it was not a living thing
and veer off just about the instant
I would swing the gun and take a shot

I never hit one never killed not even one
though for a while I would waste
a couple shells of an evening
in this so-called target practice

like I say what did I know
I was trying to find out what it meant
to be a man and part of that was work
and what you got for it

and part of that was killing which is
an education in both meat and shame
and part of all three was
what you owned up or got away with

so it took maybe another year
before anything in that vicinity
seeped past the dirt and got through to me
which happened one day a friend

gave me an ancient little gun
a breaktop .22 revolver without grips
pulled it out made a gift of it
and I was so cheered I loaded it right up

saw a bird on a fencepost eighty yards off
just a look up a snapshot
the bird drops
a shot my friend cannot believe

so we have to go and pace it off
and the bird the limp thing with
a hollowpoint through its neck
the bird turns out to be

someone I knew a catbird I admired
for performances not for my benefit
that was put out like a light
by my wanton foolishness

my friend thought it was all the gun
so accurate it was
pure magic rusty blue-black
I was overjoyed to give right back

which you have to understand
was only beginning the hard work
of sighting a gun from the muzzle
turning loose of the business end

Stocking the Lake

In return for fencing the new lake
against cattle on hot days that love
cool water under their bellies
so wade in and break down the bank
till eventually it's a mud wallow
filled in overgrown to where
it might as well never been
bulldozed to catch rain the first place

the state Wildlife Authority tells us
show up between noon and three
at the Aurora district office
with a clean empty milk can
they will give us free fish

bluegills and bass an inch long
you can practically see through
a ratio twenty to one
measured somehow by the gallon

there are more regulations
we can't fish there two years
introduce any other wildlife

so we drive all that way back
the milk can sloshing
in the trunk of Bill's old DeSoto
pour in what looks to be
handfuls of glass bluegreen slivers
that in the muddy water disappear

and keep the cattle out
though late that summer we pump
water for them till it's down to
a foot of mud among cattails

that somehow show up
so do bullfrogs water skeeters
now and again a snapping turtle
ducks dropping down the old flyway

till spring the third year
early one morning I take
a flyrod my best surface bug
with the six rubber legs and go see
what the waiting has been all about

first cast the water explodes
and I land an eight-inch bass
the mouth on him bigger than he is
unhook and release cast again
catch the same one all over
else his twin sister or brother

and that is it a lake full
as the third grade
of these scrappy little ones
panfish all the same size
who have never seen bait or hook
identical mad to be caught

and I don't fish there again

Night Stalk

It was easy just pick out
the deep twang the wide yellow
eyes in the weeds on the bank
then paddle the johnboat
with a couple planks while
one keeps the coffee can bailing
sneak in close to where a knife
lashed to the end of a sapling
stands half a chance of pinning it

the first few we hunted got away
one a bloody mess the other not a scratch
till we got the jobs sorted out
agreed which one held the light
which the homemade spear
a couple others what we called the oars
and of course the bailer
who had to be trusted
to not get excited and quit

but after a while sloshing around
in the dark we worked it out
even down to the gunny sack
and as the whole pond kept up
its gut bucket chorus
each like a bull fiddle
stuck in the mud bank
plunking its one note ga-lum
every one bellowing here-I-am
we launched our ultimate try

flailed toward the loudest and deepest
and approaching shined
light in the largest old eyes
parted cattails in a whisper
till inches off took aim and struck
straight down his gullet
while one ready reaches in grabs
tries not to cut himself

and that first purely improvised hunt
left us all one pair of
huge naked legs in the pan
kicking butter and garlic
a taste for everyone you'd think
somehow might be enough

but then within a month
we got hold of a real barbed gig
an evil steel marvel never missed
then a real boat with real oars
didn't leak a drop
and by the end of that year
there were no more jumbo bullfrogs
here the size of rabbits
brought up from Loosiana
so far back no one can remember
with only the little ones left
that had been raised to keep quiet

Making Tracks

Old guys around here got by
the Great Depression the hard way
would swear by one sure method
to bag a deer for the stewpot
without even owning a bullet

you just need a virgin snowfall
get out before dawn walk the edge of
a thicket where they bed down
pick a fresh track at first light
and follow fast as you can
all day till by sundown you come on
the deer exhausted to where
you can walk right up cut his throat
drag him home hang him up

not that we needed the meat
but at sixteen I was in shape
ran free still mostly a wild thing
got away with anything it could
hadn't yet heard how a man
shouldering his load might
clutch his chest kneel and whisper
what might be mistaken for prayer
to sense the day recede
all that sweet lightness turn rotten

so for a while without remorse
on the fly I could take any animal
watch it shiver and flail
as it sank down into its body
as if a little life were nothing more

but with only a single-shot .22
no good on big game unless
you threaded them through the eye
I listened up and thought
without a word to anyone
I might just give that a try

then was up half the night worrying
the angel dust sifting down
wouldn't stay cold enough to stick

but awoke with a jerk there it was
fresh cake icing freezing cold perfect
so I bundled up and lit out

skirted the swamp where they hide
and at daylight came on big tracks
I could tell when they sunk in
where they turned away from
low-hanging branches
must be a pretty fair buck

and the chase was on
slow motion half of it
though pretty soon I could sense
I was doing whatever he did
except sailing clean over fences
jogging thin hard patches
skittering down crickbeds
floundering drifts
sunny patches breaking through the crust

pushing to stay with him
and not sweat what I can't see
something out ahead there making tracks

so through the day I unbutton
my coat to cool off
stuff my hat in a pocket
wish I'd packed a sandwich anything
to go with the fluffy handful
I scoop up and splash in my face

not worrying noise or if
the wind's caught my scent
once I find a spot near a ridgeline
he must have stood awhile watching
me huff along there below him
from then on keeps circling downwind

which is a good sign
urges me on through the noon hour
jog a hundred paces then walk some
then another hundred on the run

lucky somewhere in there cut across
an abandoned homestead orchard
where I climb for shriveled apples
just out of his reach
chew a couple catch my second wind go on

always stuck to his tracks
never once catching sight of him
though in one thicket up ahead I seem to see
stalks and reeds bend around
something big threading its way

and by late in the day a little winded
dazed and snowblind and footsore
with one hand I can barely feel
from a glove shucked off somewhere
and a tightness in the legs lets me know
bedtime won't feel like flying

start to see signs he is slipping
meandering now as if lost

then at a steep rise when I least expect
there he is
rickety as a card table
front legs splayed

head lowered in twilight
eight sharp tines turned to meet me
watching from the corner of his eye
heaving plumes of exhaustion
smaller mangier than I'd thought

then I sidle closer
fumble all around me for the knife
but one more thing shed on the trail

look quick for something to brain him
on this downslope miles from nowhere

but there's nothing here besides
me reaching out emptyhanded
him feinting and fending off
trembling now breathing hard
dogged spent thing glaring back
in recognition
feeling the treacherous footing
as even turning to backtrack
uphill away from what's left of it
live and let live I slip and fall

III. What Anything Is Worth

What Doesn't Go in the Pot

Bright splash of one just beheaded
last burst spent zigzag crossed the yard
as if under fire

then hollowed out from craw to fundament
torn away throat's pouch of gravel
humble false teeth pocketed
to break down grain or beetle
laid open from egg in the vestibule
glowing its promise up the trail
to the faintest of her secret string of pearls

stench of her scalded and plucked
thrown to the pot with the claws on
still faintly grasping releasing

but let it end not on the platter
amid fragrant dumplings
but out in the open air

with the jacobin cap of her comb
flopped down over one eye
so alive in her precise cluck
each cluck a slight speculation
surprise huh to this huh to that
praise in her minute inspection
watching her tentative step huh
blink and nod in slow motion
wide-eyed mindful alert

to peck a living off the common ground
light on a speck whatever dropped huh
taste of another little life

Well

Rattle of chain in the pipe
short dry wait while you crank
up out of dark underfoot

to the hot tin cup taken down
from its twisted wire loop
offered the cast iron mouth

anticipating the gush
that overfills even so
splashes your legs as you lift

to the sounds of abundance
· dripping and flowing
back beneath you for the next

who feels parched
who will draw up drink deep
empty and shake out this cup

Wood Pile

Wealth in plain sight
felled green and bucked
hauled from the woods
dumped a heap in the yard
to split then stack

throw up that golden wall
built to be torn down
a chunk at a time
to be praised like food
as it is fed in the maw

that disappears in
smoke ash warmth
that radiates round the iron belly
that you slowly turn before
baking front sides back

that you spread your hands to
like a lay preacher
like a bird about to take flight
like a songbook you offer
the fire to sing of your life

Without a Word

That last week of November
some might cut off the electric
fire up the woodstove
light coal-oil lamps
sit back breathe in
a dim and flickering quiet
talk more like prayer
remind youngsters
what to be thankful about

but what of all the other
times a year some like Bill
never quite done with old ways
next day set to harvest
alfalfa clover timothy
without a word might take down
his scythe like a crookback old man
hung in the shed rafters safe

stroke with a stone till it's bright
shoulder and pace off
the corner of a field
a rough low spot where
the mower nearly always bottoms out
take a few long swipes
see does it fall and lay right
crescent swaths round his ankles
the doing rocked in its cradle
effortless no grim reaper
whispering swing low sweet chariot

reminders what had to be done
weeks on end
out of a hardscrabble youth

that he carries in offers to heifers
spilling a vast green armload
out of a whole other life

What Bill Believes

What's fair is all he'll ask
to strike a deal a hard handshake
one pump and he's done
but even with Jesus and the Indian
up on his wall side by side
nowdays he won't go to church

though sometimes Sunday nights
he will go up the road where
a neighbor who's not a bad farmer
though he's been driven to log
his hardwoods to pay taxes
has some people in

self-taught evangelical
pentecostal somesuch
still gets pretty worked up
when the mood takes him
there in his own parlor
falls down babbles in tongues

but when I ask what Bill believes
he says God speaks to him
in the quiet in the hot sun
that like the land runs on and on
that in the dark cicadas and peepers
can't help interrupting

Interlopers

In the night behind the stove
this time of year
around baseboards woodbox the pantry
like a miniature racetrack
you will hear them scampering

restless just in from the fields
the first cold snap
like whiskered iron filings
drawn by a magnet
squeak through the tiniest crack

somehow slip under the door
around the overfed cat
practically straight through the dog
steal his chow
unaware of the meaning of fear

since the oldest among them recalls
how all around us
plenty falls to the floor
that is theirs if only they locate
a snug warm hole and stay quiet

pretend not to even be here
but somehow like kids they can never
contain their exuberance
the instant we put the light out
start up their own county fair

acrobats dangle and drop
into anything they want a look at
suspect of a hint of nourishment
leave toothmarks on toothpaste
trail musty droppings all over

bother us up out of bed to where
we bait traps with a taste of the good stuff
that unless they cracked the old icebox
with its crumbling rubber gasket
we might never otherwise share

Inventory

These windswept chilly grey days
with no more leafy distractions
from bones still hard to look at
that have been here all along
sometimes you pull rubber boots on

roam stubble fields muddy lanes
visit what's emptied undone
through orchard to woodlot
barn to pasture outbuildings
shed to stalls to what have you

skirt swollen pond poke around
scrap lumber pile nearly compost
climb hayloft counting bales
walk fencelines frozen crickbed
puzzle snow tracks humble tales

then tromp indoors toss aside
muffler mittens and knitcap
dig the cakes off your bootsoles
wonder what's cooking pitch in
peeling freshdug potatoes

then after dinner pull up
a straightbacked chair
a new pad and pencil
turn up the lamp at your elbow
to figure close as you dare

recall what's been turned under
what petered out and what thrived
calculate what's on hand
tally the willing then divine
like as not what's to come

what needs you can supply
what hurts mend
what's failed you have to leave
well enough alone to heal itself
scar the back of your hand

seeing as how precious little
can be absolutely counted on
still and all someone has to
say never mind what folks crave
what do we plant that will grow here

then later with eyes closed in bed
again wander margins wherever
desires unmapped still elude you
dream newborn animals frolic
fields spring unbidden to life

Come the Dark of the Year

Come the dark of the year when
underlit wings wheeling head for home
when ruts in furrowed ground
yesterday poured full of sky
now reflect nothing
glazed over empty-eyed

comes time to hunker down into
what little is left to be done
keep the kettle on the livestock in
the wish-book out
the covers tucked
the firewood coming

retell those tales one winter where
locked in ice
the means of life ran low
they tore out walls to burn
dragged in planks from the barn
splintered perfectly decent furniture

ate up all they had put by
share and share alike
in shallow spoonfuls down
to cattle feed from the trough
until the sun rose to greet them
its measureless warmth just in time

Out of Retirement

Old farmers yarnspin around
the woodstove back of the store
chairs leaned away on two legs

make a mess of the floor
whittling down through
the longest night of the year

cram another log on
watch through mica windows
white heat falter take hold

start speculating old problems
what they ought to have done
not take the loss on that feed corn

complain how they feel lately
each change in the weather
flex stiff knee swollen knuckle

get to telling jokes known to
everyone and his cousin
but for the new kid all ears

watching to see should he laugh
then a break in the banter
palms offered studying shadows

silence goes weaving together
flickering thick blue air
till someone leans forward

no damn good reason
youth called out of retirement
maybe one last look

out through a lost front tooth
spits tobacco juice
onto the dull glowing

stovelid an instant
burnt whiff dancing sizzle
joke of a life up in smoke

Sharpening

In bright light you approach
the nothingness of the edge
a painstaking lick at a time
stroke away until gleaming
nicks and ridges disappear

but before long learn use dulls
that you have to return
work down one side then the other
outward toward infinity moreover
reckon how age eats the tool

even treated right cleaned
and oiled to a fare-thee-well
over time tools pass beyond use
to where they hang back untouched
nailed to shadows of themselves

most have had a shovel that
losing the point of its tongue
eventually wears to
a wavering smirk and a bite
that's all or nothing

that gets too tough to work
its way back into dirt
so gets to lean and linger
while a knife licked away
by a whetstone retreats till

cutting a slice your knuckles
hit the breadboard
well in advance of the blade
and the last of every cut
has to be torn off the loaf

Subsistence

First you might have whittled
a noggin out of a burl
to hang by a belt loop
to scoop and lift yourself a drink of water

then sometime buy a tin cup
to hang by the well still offering
a drink that anyone could share
till water was piped indoors

where each cup at last would be washed
decorative fragile or better
made of paper used once thrown away
no sweet song of sanitation

and surely no marching song
of civilization on the rise
mostly a groan of expediency
a harmonic of profit and loss

ignored until someone gets thirsty

2

In the days before indoor plumbing
central heating electric
hot and cold running anything

before matching cabinets
walk-in closets
much less air-conditioning

in the days of trunks linen chests
haylofts rootcellars attics
almost before keys in locks

when all water would have to be pumped
carried in sloshing on floorboards
when rugs were rolled back for the dance

twice a year wrestled out
hung up and beaten in daylight
when in season everyone would smell faintly

of the damp essence of work
when everyone knew and accepted
welcomed what that meant

3

You always figure cash crops close
tobacco that strip of prime bottom
milk cows daily output
alfalfa mustard or turnip seed
so fine you run a comb through
even butter and egg money
whatever proves a sure profit

for though young Lincoln worked his sums
on a shovel with charcoal by firelight
one winter tied elm bark on his feet for shoes
increasingly things can't be traded
or made from scratch
beyond pencils eyeglasses school books
medicines gasoline microchips

4

But sure as we kept and maintained
a baler and thresh machine
the farm had a shoe last
nearby boxed hobnails and heels
beeswax an awl glue and leather scraps
the farm had yardgoods by the bolt
in two-three basic colors

to feed the treadle sewing machine
for near anything can be fashioned
from what's at hand
down to a vest and coveralls
and nothing is ever thrown out
threadbare scraps you quilt
summer dress a patterned flour sack

and in the pantry churn and canning jars
in the drawer to join whatever broke
leather punch brass rivet
on the bench clamps a jack a come-along
scraps of bailing wire twine
to make you hold still for the trimming
chainsaw hair clippers take your pick

5

And along the south side of the house
of course the vegetable garden
miniature farm grown only for ourselves
where we planted whatever we wanted
where long evenings after work

we would water hoe and pull weeds
watched over by the scarecrow
every summer new-made
of donated hand-me-downs
so bore that family resemblance

with everything but the labor
of breaking ground done by hand
where patches would migrate around
crops in an ancient procession
through the long growing season

singing their litany
lettuce greens carrots peas beans
squash melons sweetcorn tomatoes
cabbage beets pumpkins potatoes
all of it fresh and all free

6

Not to mention the dappled mown
yard that is mostly orchard
with grapevines on a high arbor
so you can walk in their shade
a berry patch down the fenceline

and by the house beds of tulips
near the tree-swing the lilacs
and climbing up a trellis by the door
some variety of tea rose
planted now a hundred years and more

7

With weather shifts growth and loss
the promise of work all four seasons
though money only once

the question used to be how to balance
bad years of little or nothing
with the good when you might be paid back

now regular as clockwork
comes the interest on the debt
and every fall hat in hand you show up

to wait to be told your business
by one dressed up for a funeral
who speaks bottom lines what things cost

which you nod and accept
otherwise work for wages
hire someone to shingle your barn

when in the off-season
you could throw up that scaffold
tear off and nail down yourself

8

Still even barn dances it beckons
where you once might have plucked out a tune
town kids mock hightop work shoes
drive cars worth a good man's year's wages
brag they could never fix anything
for the exercise lift shiny weights

and cackling over the boom box
label things folks and doings
farmer like it's a dirty word
as if working caring for the land
were not all we mean by independence
character substance and worth

9

No one wants to go back
to take up the hard old ways
to give the rough road we have come
more than a moment's glance
over the shoulder through
wavy glass cobwebs flyspecks

though much of that world is still there
in corners rusting unused
heaps of rank reminiscence
too much work to throw out
piled up mouldering waiting
to be examined and weighed

for what is anything worth
but the sweat I put into it
plus the gift of the soil
enough sun and rain in good time
minus what the birds eat
rabbits and squirrels their entitlement

and who cannot figure the value
of a person by what he will lend
give or help out with
should trouble come knocking
some dark night out of nowhere
with nobody's given name on it

Feel Your Way

Work unfinished as always
let go a lick before you
blundered broke something

now sit on the porch
face and hands rinsed
shoes kicked away

shirt fluttering as sweat dries
picking guitar thinking nothing
as light fades night climbs

notes knock at windows
swirl beneath evergreens
echo the last sounds of day

and as night stirs alive
awakening sings old desires
you rise up pitch-dark at last

feel your way in light the lamp
stoke the stove for leftovers
slice bread ladle out a bowl

sit head bowed a moment
over how this ordinary day
scarce a cloud in the sky

has come out even
down to scooping a bellyful
down to the pause to let cool

Author's Note

For a long time I thought I had only one note, the elegaic—speaking well at funerals, barefoot in the rubble of the past. But then realized that was a stall, a dodge, and getting on with one's life entails savoring the present moment while squishing one's toes in the muck of history, smacking one's lips over the memorable meal, praising what the cook forgot to season, singing even on an empty stomach. And further, piling crib and love-nest and sickbed with music and jokes and stories and edible tidbits—all of which go into making good poems, that together might conjure the world to come, the world lost.

So I endlessly seek ways to let the life within greet the life without us. Reaching behind and ahead. And admit to a craving in each piece to make the reader laugh and cry, and do a few steps of the dance.

Colophon

The text and display types of this edition are set in Adobe Jenson, a faithful electronic version of the 1470 roman face of Nicolas Jenson. Legend has it that Jenson, a Frenchman employed as the mintmaster at Tours, was sent to Mainz in 1458 by Charles VII to learn the new art of printing in the shop of Gutenberg, and import it to France. But he never returned, next appearing in Venice in 1468. Type historian Daniel Berkeley Updike praises the Jenson Roman for "its readability, its mellowness of form, and the evenness of color in mass." Updike concludes, "Jenson's roman types have been the accepted models for roman letters ever since he made them, and, repeatedly copied in our own day, have never been equalled." The type used for the front cover is Legacy. The designer is Ronald Arnholm (born 1939). He was first inspired to create the typeface when in a type history class, he was impressed by a copy of the 1470 edition of Eusebius, set in the roman type of Nicolas Jenson. Arnholm went on to create a revival of Jenson's work, now called Jenson Roman, also in the Linotype Library. The type used for the back cover is Adobe Jenson.

Silverfish Review Press is committed to preserving ancient forests and natural resources. We elected to print *Ripening* on 50% post consumer recycled paper, processed chlorine free. As a result, for this printing, we have saved: 1 tree (40' tall and 6-8" diameter), 385 gallons of water, 155 kilowatt hours of electricity, 42 pounds of solid waste, and 83 pounds of greenhouse gases. Thomson-Shore, Inc. is a member of Green Press Initiative, a nonprofit program dedicated to supporting authors, publishers, and suppliers in their efforts to reduce their use of fiber obtained from endangered forests. For more information, visit www.greenpressinitiative.org.

Cover design by Valerie Brewster, Scribe Typography.
Text design by Rodger Moody and Connie Kudura, ProtoType Graphics.
Printed on acid-free papers and bound by Thomson-Shore, Inc.